THE JPS B'NAI MITZVAH TORAH COMMENTARY

Ki Tavo' (Deuteronomy 26:1–29:8)
Haftarah (Isaiah 60:1–22)

Rabbi Jeffrey K. Salkin

T0335309

The Jewish Publication Society · Philadelphia
University of Nebraska Press · Lincoln

INTRODUCTION

News flash: the most important thing about becoming bar or bat mitzvah isn't the party. Nor is it the presents. Nor even being able to celebrate with your family and friends—as wonderful as those things are. Nor is it even standing before the congregation and reading the prayers of the liturgy—as important as that is.

No, the most important thing about becoming bar or bat mitzvah is sharing Torah with the congregation. And why is that? Because of all Jewish skills, that is the most important one.

Here is what is true about rites of passage: you can tell what a culture values by the tasks it asks its young people to perform on their way to maturity. In American culture, you become responsible for driving, responsible for voting, and yes, responsible for drinking responsibly.

In some cultures, the rite of passage toward maturity includes some kind of trial, or a test of strength. Sometimes, it is a kind of "outward bound" camping adventure. Among the Maasai tribe in Africa, it is traditional for a young person to hunt and kill a lion. In some Hispanic cultures, fifteen year-old girls celebrate the *quinceañera*, which marks their entrance into maturity.

What is Judaism's way of marking maturity? It combines both of these rites of passage: *responsibility* and *test*. You show that you are on your way to becoming a *responsible* Jewish adult through a public *test* of strength and knowledge—reading or chanting Torah, and then teaching it to the congregation.

This is the most important Jewish ritual mitzvah (commandment), and that is how you demonstrate that you are, truly, bar or bat mitzvah—old enough to be responsible for the mitzvot.

What Is Torah?

So, what exactly is the Torah? You probably know this already, but let's review.

The Torah (teaching) consists of "the five books of Moses," sometimes also called the *chumash* (from the Hebrew word *chameish,* which means "five"), or, sometimes, the Greek word Pentateuch (which means "the five teachings").

Here are the five books of the Torah, with their common names and their Hebrew names.

> **Genesis (The beginning), which in Hebrew is Bere'shit (from the first words—"When God began to create").** Bere'shit spans the years from Creation to Joseph's death in Egypt. Many of the Bible's best stories are in Genesis: the creation story itself; Adam and Eve in the Garden of Eden; Cain and Abel; Noah and the Flood; and the tales of the Patriarchs and Matriarchs, Abraham, Isaac, Jacob, Sarah, Rebekah, Rachel, and Leah. It also includes one of the greatest pieces of world literature, the story of Joseph, which is actually the oldest complete novel in history, comprising more than one-quarter of all Genesis.

> **Exodus (Getting out), which in Hebrew is Shemot (These are the names).** Exodus begins with the story of the Israelite slavery in Egypt. It then moves to the rise of Moses as a leader, and the Israelites' liberation from slavery. After the Israelites leave Egypt, they experience the miracle of the parting of the Sea of Reeds (or "Red Sea"); the giving of the Ten Commandments at Mount Sinai; the idolatry of the Golden Calf; and the design and construction of the Tabernacle and of the ark for the original tablets of the law, which our ancestors carried with them in the desert. Exodus also includes various ethical and civil laws, such as "You shall not wrong a stranger or oppress him, for you were strangers in the land of Egypt" (22:20).

> **Leviticus (about the Levites), or, in Hebrew, Va-yikra' (And God called).** It goes into great detail about the kinds of sacrifices that the ancient Israelites brought as offerings; the laws of ritual purity; the animals that were permitted and forbidden for eating (the beginnings of the tradition of kashrut, the Jewish dietary laws); the diagnosis of various skin diseases; the ethical laws of holiness; the ritual calendar of the Jewish year; and various agricultural laws concerning the treatment of the Land of Israel. Leviticus is basically the manual of ancient Judaism.

> Numbers (because the book begins with the census of the Isra-
> elites), or, in Hebrew, Be-midbar (In the wilderness). The book
> describes the forty years of wandering in the wilderness and the
> various rebellions against Moses. The constant theme: "Egypt
> wasn't so bad. Maybe we should go back." The greatest rebellion
> against Moses was the negative reports of the spies about the
> Land of Israel, which discouraged the Israelites from wanting to
> move forward into the land. For that reason, the "wilderness gen-
> eration" must die off before a new generation can come into ma-
> turity and finish the journey.
>
> Deuteronomy (The repetition of the laws of the Torah), or, in
> Hebrew, Devarim (The words). The final book of the Torah is,
> essentially, Moses's farewell address to the Israelites as they pre-
> pare to enter the Land of Israel. Here we find various laws that
> had been previously taught, though sometimes with different
> wording. Much of Deuteronomy contains laws that will be im-
> portant to the Israelites as they enter the Land of Israel—laws
> concerning the establishment of a monarchy and the ethics of
> warfare. Perhaps the most famous passage from Deuteronomy
> contains the *Shema*, the declaration of God's unity and unique-
> ness, and the *Ve-ahavta*, which follows it. Deuteronomy ends with
> the death of Moses on Mount Nebo as he looks across the Jordan
> Valley into the land that he will not enter.

Jews read the Torah in sequence—starting with Bere'shit right after Simchat Torah in the autumn, and then finishing Devarim on the
following Simchat Torah. Each Torah portion is called a parashah (di-
vision; sometimes called a *sidrah,* a place in the order of the Torah
reading). The stories go around in a full circle, reminding us that we
can always gain more insights and more wisdom from the Torah. This
means that if you don't "get" the meaning this year, don't worry—it
will come around again.

And What Else? The Haftarah

We read or chant the Torah from the Torah scroll—the most sacred
thing that a Jewish community has in its possession. The Torah is

written without vowels, and the ability to read it and chant it is part of the challenge and the test.

But there is more to the synagogue reading. Every Torah reading has an accompanying haftarah reading. Haftarah means "conclusion," because there was once a time when the service actually ended with that reading. Some scholars believe that the reading of the haftarah originated at a time when non-Jewish authorities outlawed the reading of the Torah, and the Jews read the haftarah sections instead. In fact, in some synagogues, young people who become bar or bat mitzvah read very little Torah and instead read the entire haftarah portion.

The haftarah portion comes from the Nevi'im, the prophetic books, which are the second part of the Jewish Bible. It is either read or chanted from a Hebrew Bible, or maybe from a booklet or a photocopy.

The ancient sages chose the haftarah passages because their themes reminded them of the words or stories in the Torah text. Sometimes, they chose *haftarah* with special themes in honor of a festival or an upcoming festival.

Not all books in the prophetic section of the Hebrew Bible consist of prophecy. Several are historical. For example:

The book of Joshua tells the story of the conquest and settlement of Israel.

The book of Judges speaks of the period of early tribal rulers who would rise to power, usually for the purpose of uniting the tribes in war against their enemies. Some of these leaders are famous: Deborah, the great prophetess and military leader, and Samson, the biblical strong man.

The books of Samuel start with Samuel, the last judge, and then move to the creation of the Israelite monarchy under Saul and David (approximately 1000 BCE).

The books of Kings tell of the death of King David, the rise of King Solomon, and how the Israelite kingdom split into the Northern Kingdom of Israel and the Southern Kingdom of Judah (approximately 900 BCE).

And then there are the books of the prophets, those spokesmen for God whose words fired the Jewish conscience. Their names are immortal: Isaiah, Jeremiah, Ezekiel, Amos, Hosea, among others.

Someone once said: "There is no evidence of a biblical prophet ever being invited back a second time for dinner." Why? Because the prophets were tough. They had no patience for injustice, apathy, or hypocrisy. No one escaped their criticisms. Here's what they taught:

> God commands the Jews to behave decently toward one another. In fact, God cares more about basic ethics and decency than about ritual behavior.
> God chose the Jews *not* for special privileges, but for special duties to humanity.
> As bad as the Jews sometimes were, there was always the possibility that they would improve their behavior.
> As bad as things might be now, it will not always be that way. Someday, there will be universal justice and peace. Human history is moving forward toward an ultimate conclusion that some call the Messianic Age: a time of universal peace and prosperity for the Jewish people and for all the people of the world.

Your Mission—To Teach Torah to the Congregation

On the day when you become bar or bat mitzvah, you will be reading, or chanting, Torah—in Hebrew. You will be reading, or chanting, the haftarah—in Hebrew. That is the major skill that publicly marks the becoming of bar or bat mitzvah. But, perhaps even more important than that, you need to be able to teach something about the Torah portion, and perhaps the haftarah as well.

And that is where this book comes in. It will be a very valuable resource for you, and your family, in the b'nai mitzvah process.

Here is what you will find in it:

> A brief **summary** of every Torah portion. This is a basic overview of the portion; and, while it might not refer to everything in the Torah portion, it will explain its most important aspects.
> A list of the **major ideas** in the Torah portion. The purpose: to make the Torah portion real, in ways that we can relate to. Every Torah portion contains unique ideas, and when you put all

of those ideas together, you actually come up with a list of Judaism's most important ideas.

› Two ***divrei Torah*** ("words of Torah," or "sermonettes") for each portion. These *divrei Torah* explain significant aspects of the Torah portion in accessible, reader-friendly language. Each *devar Torah* contains references to **traditional** Jewish sources (those that were written before the modern era), as well as **modern** sources and quotes. We have searched, far and wide, to find sources that are unusual, interesting, and not just the "same old stuff" that many people already know about the Torah portion. Why did we include these minisermons in the volume? Not because we want you to simply copy those sermons and pass them off as your own (that would be cheating), though you are free to quote from them. We included them so that you can see what is possible—how you can try to make meaning for yourself out of the words of Torah.

› **Connections:** This is perhaps the most valuable part. It's a list of questions that you can ask yourself, or that others might help you think about—any of which can lead to the creation of your *devar Torah.*

Note: you don't have to like everything that's in a particular Torah portion. Some aren't that loveable. Some are hard to understand; some are about religious practices that people today might find confusing, and even offensive; some contain ideas that we might find totally outmoded.

But this doesn't have to get in the way. After all, most kids spend a lot of time thinking about stories that contain ideas that modern people would find totally bizarre. Any good medieval fantasy story falls into that category.

And we also believe that, if you spend just a little bit of time with those texts, you can begin to understand what the author was trying to say.

This volume goes one step further. Sometimes, the haftarah comes off as a second thought, and no one really thinks about it. We have tried to solve that problem by including a **summary** of each haftarah, and then a mini-sermon on the haftarah. This will help you learn how these sacred words are relevant to today's world, and even to your own life.

All Bible quotations come from the NJPS translation, which is found in the many different editions of the JPS TANAKH; in the Conservative movement's *Etz Hayim: Torah and Commentary;* in the Reform movement's *Torah: A Modern Commentary;* and in other Bible commentaries and study guides.

How Do I Write a *Devar Torah?*

It really is easier than it looks.

There are many ways of thinking about the *devar Torah.* It is, of course, a short sermon on the meaning of the Torah (and, perhaps, the haftarah) portion. It might even be helpful to think of the *devar Torah* as a "book report" on the portion itself.

The most important thing you can know about this sacred task is: *Learn* the words. *Love* the words. Teach people what it could mean to *live* the words.

Here's a basic outline for a *devar Torah:*

"My Torah portion is (name of portion) _____,
   from the book of _____, chapter
   _____.

"In my Torah portion, we learn that_____
   (Summary of portion)
"For me, the most important lesson of this Torah portion is (what
   is the best thing in the portion? Take the portion as a whole;
   your *devar Torah* does not have to be only, or specifically, on the
   verses that you are reading).
"As I learned my Torah portion, I found myself wondering:
   ‣ *Raise a question that the Torah portion itself raises.*
   ‣ *"Pick a fight"* with the portion. Argue with it.
   ‣ *Answer a question* that is listed in the "Connections" section of
     each Torah portion.
   ‣ *Suggest a question to your rabbi* that you would want the rabbi
     to answer in his or her own *devar Torah* or sermon.

"I have lived the values of the Torah by _____
(here, you can talk about how the Torah portion relates to your
own life. If you have done a mitzvah project, you can talk about
that here).

How To Keep It from Being Boring
(and You from Being Bored)

Some people just don't like giving traditional speeches. From our perspective, that's really okay. Perhaps you can teach Torah in a different way—one that makes sense to you.

> Write an "open letter" to one of the characters in your Torah portion. "Dear Abraham: I hope that your trip to Canaan was not too hard . . ." "Dear Moses: Were you afraid when you got the Ten Commandments on Mount Sinai? I sure would have been . . ."
> Write a news story about what happens. Imagine yourself to be a television or news reporter. "Residents of neighboring cities were horrified yesterday as the wicked cities of Sodom and Gomorrah were burned to the ground. Some say that God was responsible . . ."
> Write an imaginary interview with a character in your Torah portion.
> Tell the story from the point of view of another character, or a minor character, in the story. For instance, tell the story of the Garden of Eden from the point of view of the serpent. Or the story of the Binding of Isaac from the point of view of the ram, which was substituted for Isaac as a sacrifice. Or perhaps the story of the sale of Joseph from the point of view of his coat, which was stripped off him and dipped in a goat's blood.
> Write a poem about your Torah portion.
> Write a song about your Torah portion.
> Write a play about your Torah portion, and have some friends act it out with you.
> Create a piece of artwork about your Torah portion.

The bottom line is: Make this a joyful experience. Yes—it could even be fun.

The Very Last Thing You Need to Know at This Point

The Torah scroll is written without vowels. Why? Don't *sofrim* (Torah scribes) know the vowels?

Of course they do.

So, why do they leave the vowels out?

One reason is that the Torah came into existence at a time when sages were still arguing about the proper vowels, and the proper pronunciation.

But here is another reason: The Torah text, as we have it today, and as it sits in the scroll, is actually *an unfinished work*. Think of it: the words are just sitting there. Because they have no vowels, it is as if they have no voice.

When we read the Torah publicly, we give voice to the ancient words. And when we find meaning in those ancient words, and we talk about those meanings, those words jump to life. They enter our lives. They make our world deeper and better.

Mazal tov to you, and your family. This is your journey toward Jewish maturity. Love it.

THE TORAH

❖ Ki Tavo': Deuteronomy 26:1–29:8

Parashat Ki Tavo' continues the theme of social justice that is such a major part of Deuteronomy. It describes three rituals that Israelites, both as individuals and as an entire community, had to perform upon entrance into the Land of Israel. Each of those rituals expresses gratitude at having arrived in the land, but they tie that gratitude to a sense of memory—of where the Israelites have come from, and the circumstances that have produced their history.

The Torah portion ends with a ghastly passage: a list of the catastrophes that would befall the Jewish people if they failed to abide by the covenant.

Summary

> An Israelite must present his or her first fruits from the harvest, put them in a basket, and place it on the altar. He or she must then recite an autobiographical statement, which recounts Israelite history up to that point, and in which the Israelite fully identifies with the experience of slavery in Egypt and in being freed from slavery. This ceremony is known as *vidui bikkurim* (the confession or proclamation of the first fruits) and was originally performed on the ancient *Chag ha-Bikkurim* (The festival of the first fruits), which was the original version of the festival that we know as Shavuot. This whole passage forms the core of the narrative in the Passover Haggadah. (26:1–11)

> A second ritual: every third year, Israelites must set aside the tithe (ten percent) of their yield, and they must give it to the Levite, the stranger, the fatherless, and the widow. (26:12–15)

> A third ritual: this time to mark the Israelites' eventual entry into the Land of Israel. The Israelites divide up into their individual tribes and stand on two facing mountains—Mount Gerizim and Mount Ebal. They recite a list of things that are to be prohibited and therefore cursed, which is followed by the blessings that will occur if those prohibitions are observed. (27:11–28:14)

> Now comes one of the worst (if not the worst) passages in the entire Torah: Moses tells the Israelites exactly what will happen to them if they fail to live by the covenant with God. The punishments include exile, pestilence, illness, starvation, blight, mildew, a lack of rain, defeat by Israel's enemies, total despair, and madness. It only gets worse. It is not pretty. (28:15–68)

The Big Ideas

> **To be Jewish means to locate yourself within the larger Jewish story.** In many ways, wherever Jews go and whatever Jews do, the past walks with them. For that reason, the text of the *vidui bikkurim* forms the central part of the Passover Haggadah. It is the story of a people who have been liberated from slavery and allowed to celebrate in freedom. To quote the Jewish poet A. M. Klein: "generations look through our eyes."

> **When Jews celebrate, they must remember those who are less fortunate.** The passage from Deuteronomy imagines that the Israelites who tithe have already become prosperous. The tithe reminds us that Jews must give to the most vulnerable in society. While it would be great to imagine a society without those who are poor and on the fringes, the Torah is very realistic about how society works. Such people will always be with us, and therefore we will always have responsibilities to them.

> **Actions have consequences.** This is one of the most important things that people learn as they grow into maturity, and this is what the ancient Israelites had to learn as well. If you do bad things, bad stuff will happen. If you do good things, good stuff will happen. It is interesting to note that the list of prohibitions in this Torah portion consists of sins that are mainly committed in private, which reminds us that everything we do is part of our moral and spiritual makeup. Moreover, while some laws contained in the list can be found elsewhere in the Torah (especially the laws about sexual behaviors), some are new—like moving a neighbor's landmark, which basically meant trespassing on someone else's property. Finally, in place of the original Ten Commandments (Exodus 20), here there are twelve—a number that reminds us of the twelve tribes of ancient Israel.

> **Societies that ignore ethics will inevitably fall apart.** This is a constant theme in the Torah. Noah's generation did evil; it was punished with the Flood. The people of Sodom and Gomorrah did evil; they were punished by destruction. And so it would be for the People of Israel as well—failure to observe the rules of the Torah would

result in the destruction of their nation. In fact, the catastrophic things that are described in this Torah portion actually did happen to the Jewish people during the Assyrian exile (721 BCE) and the Babylonian exile (586 BCE). Many scholars, therefore, believe that these passages might have been written in the wake of that latter disaster, and represent an attempt on the part of the Jewish people to give reasons for the tragedy. If such a terrible thing happened, it must have been our fault, so let's clean up our act.

Divrei Torah

WHO ARE YOU, REALLY?

A rabbi in a Philadelphia suburb wants to add the following ritual to bar and bat mitzvah ceremonies at her synagogue: At the celebration after the service, each kid must take the first gifts that he or she has received, put them in a large basket, and put the basket on a centrally located table. Then, the child must go through his or her entire family history, as far as he or she knows it. For example: "My great-grandfather came from Poland, and he left there because the Jews were persecuted. He came to Philadelphia, and lived in a neighborhood called Strawberry Mansion. Then, my grandfather moved out to northeast Philadelphia. And then, my parents moved out to the Main Line. And now, I am here, and I am grateful for all that I have."

That was essentially what happened in the ancient ritual known as *vidui bikkurim,* the confession or proclamation of the first fruits. The Mishnah describes the joyous ceremony in which people traveled to Jerusalem: "Those who lived near Jerusalem brought fresh figs and grapes, but those from a distance brought dried figs and raisins. An ox with horns bedecked with gold and with an olive crown on its head led the way. The flute was played before them until they got close to Jerusalem. . . . When they reached the Temple Mount, even King Agrippa would take the basket and place it on his shoulder and walk as far as the temple court." Why does it say "even" King Agrippa? Because even though he was a king, he still recalled his humble origins.

For the Jews, memory is key—and no biblical book mentions memory more than Deuteronomy. Memory is mentioned 169 times in the Torah (which is 13 x 13, the age of bar or bat mitzvah, squared). As the author Yosef Hayim Yerushalmi has written: "Only in Israel and nowhere else is the injunction to remember felt as a religious imperative to an entire people."

Memory carries with it a sense of obligation, not merely curiosity and nostalgia. Memory creates identity: it means locating your brief life within a larger context and within a story that gives it meaning and direction.

But, go back to the Torah text and read it again (26:5–9). It talks about the Patriarchs, and about slavery, and about entering the Land of Israel. What is missing from the sacred recitation? The revelation of Torah and the forty years of wandering in the wilderness.

Memory is selective. No history book can include everything that happened, just as no Facebook page can capture the totality of a person's life. As you get older, you will remember many things that happened. But you will also forget many things that happened. Some things you might even want to forget. After all, not everything can be important.

Just remember where you come from, who made you, who you are; and be grateful!

ARE YOU AN ARAMEAN?

There was an old television show called *The Lone Ranger*. The Lone Ranger was a hero in the Old West, and he wore a mask to conceal his identity. Whenever he would leave the scene, people would ask each other: "Who was that masked man?"

It is time to ask that question once again. The declaration of the first fruits begins with the Israelites saying: *Arami oved avi*, "My father was a fugitive Aramean" (26:5). The Rabbis were intrigued: why would the important declaration begin with that strange sentence? What does it mean? Just who was this ancestor?

The region in which the Arameans lived was ancient Mesopotamia, which was where the Jewish nation originated. Abraham was (sort of) an Aramean. So, the "fugitive Aramean" would be Abraham. Abraham's grandson Jacob also came from that region (when he sought refuge from his brother, Esau), and, as the Torah says, he certainly did come down into Egypt and he flourished there. So, the "fugitive Aramean" might also have been Jacob.

Not so fast. This passage from the Torah portion appears prominently in the Passover Haggadah. And, there, the Aramean is actually someone else: Laban—Rebecca's brother, Rachel and Leah's father, and Jacob's father-in-law. The verb *oved*, which means "fugitive" or "wandering," can also mean "destroy." That is how the Haggadah understands it: "Go and learn what Laban the Aramean sought to do to Jacob. Pharaoh only decreed the death of the males. Laban sought to destroy them all."

Why would the Haggadah make such a harsh statement about Laban, who was, after all, a close relative of biblical Matriarchs and a Patriarch?

Recall that when Jacob falls in love with Laban's daughter Rachel Laban tricks Jacob and gives him his older daughter, Leah, instead. Why? "It is not the practice in our place to marry off the younger before the older" (Gen. 29:26). Talk about sleazy! He tricks Jacob, and when his trick is discovered, he invokes local custom and "tradition." He doesn't care at all about Jacob's feelings, or even those of his daughter Rachel (and probably not of Leah either). Jacob must work another seven years in order to marry Rachel.

Years later, Jacob wants to take his family and leave Laban's household. They leave in the middle of the night, and Laban chases after them. Is it because he just wanted to kiss them all goodbye? Actually, no. It was because his household idols were missing and he suspects Jacob of taking them (actually, it was Rachel who stole them—check out the story in Genesis 31). Laban doesn't really care that much about his family leaving him. He's mostly concerned about his missing idols.

Laban doesn't care that much about people or relationships. And he really doesn't care that much about his family; he's only worried that someone might have taken something from him.

If Jacob thought and acted the way that Laban did, it would have shattered his family, and it would have implanted feelings of selfishness within the Jewish people. Instead, Laban's actions may have reminded Jacob of his own trickery against his brother, and spurred him to do the right thing and reconcile with Esau.

As the modern Bible teacher Nehama Leibowitz teaches: "The Jewish people had a special obligation, to remember with gratitude, that they had been delivered from a foreign soil and had been brought to their own land."

So we need to remember our Aramean origins in more ways than one: Abraham, Jacob, and Laban—the good and the bad.

Connections

> ‣ Do you know aspects of your family's history, going back beyond your grandparents? Do you know where your family is from? What do you know about them, and what could that mean to you?
> ‣ Why is it important for people to tithe—giving ten percent to charity or for a good cause that you believe in? Is that ten percent figure still practical today? What charities or causes are you passionate about?
> ‣ How have you succeeded (or not succeeded) in keeping away from bad influences?
> ‣ Why do you think that Jews have a particular fondness for (and talent for) memory?
> ‣ Do you think that gratitude is a good value? What are you most grateful for? How do you demonstrate it?

THE HAFTARAH

❖ Ki Tavo': Isaiah 60:1–22

As the clock ticks, and as it gets closer to Rosh Hashanah, it looks ever more likely that God will keep the divine promise and restore the Jewish people to their homeland. That is the triumphant mood of this haftarah. It is filled with images of light, which in Judaism are always synonymous with Torah, God, and hope itself.

Not only will the Jews be brought back to their land; other nations will come to serve them, and those that refuse to do so will vanish. Things will be so good for the Jews that even nature will conspire to help them; the people will no longer need either the light of the sun, or that of the moon.

The Secret of Judaism's Most Popular Song

Imagine if Judaism had a "greatest hits" list; what would be its most popular song?

The answer: *Lekhah Dodi,* the hymn that is sung on Erev Shabbat. There are thousands of versions of this song, and it seems that Jewish composers are writing new versions every year.

Lekhah Dodi emerged from the city of Safed, in the north of Israel. In the sixteenth century, Safed consisted of a small community of mystical seekers, most of them refugees from Spain. Many of those mystical seekers gathered around a charismatic teacher, Rabbi Isaac Luria.

Solomon ha-Levi Alkabetz was part of Luria's "club," and he was the author of *Lekhah Dodi.* In the song Alkabetz imagines that Shabbat is a bride—and that when Jews observe Shabbat, it is as if they actually "marry" Shabbat. The opening line and refrain is: "Come, my friend, to meet the bride; let us welcome the presence of the Sabbath." As Luria himself wrote: "I sing in hymns to enter the gates of the field of apples of holy ones. A new table we lay for her, a beautiful candelabrum sheds its light upon us. Between right and left the bride approaches in holy jewels and festive garments. . . . Torment and cries are past. Now there are new faces and souls and spirits."

When Alkabetz wrote *Lekhah Dodi*, he freely picked verses from the prophet Second Isaiah—in particular, this week's haftarah portion: "Arise, shine, for your light has dawned; the Presence of the Lord has shone upon you!" (60:1)

What's the connection between Second Isaiah's vision of redemption and Shabbat?

Here's what is happening. As we have seen, Second Isaiah is obsessed with the Jews' return to the Land of Israel, and, in particular, Jerusalem. For Jews, Jerusalem is the holiest place in the world, and Shabbat is the holiest time in the week. It all fits together. The holiness of place combines with the holiness of time—two "Shabbats" coming together. That is why the Talmud teaches: "If only Israel would observe just two *Shabbatot,* then they would immediately be redeemed."

For weeks, the prophet has been urging the Jews: Stop mourning for Jerusalem and the Land of Israel; it's almost time to come home! In the words of Professor Reuven Kimmelman: "The task of the singer of 'Lekhah Dodi' is to comfort the mourning city and to urge her to get up from sitting shivah. He reassures her that the original beloved bridegroom who abandoned her will be back and now it is time to ready herself for his return."

And just as mourning for Jerusalem must end, Shabbat symbolizes the temporary postponing of mourning. You can't mourn on Shabbat. In the synagogue, as the singing of *Lekhah Dodi* ends, it is customary for the community to welcome that week's mourners into the synagogue. The traditional greeting combines personal and national comfort: "May God comfort you, among all those who mourn for Zion and Jerusalem."

So the imminent return of the Jews from exile will be like a never-ending Shabbat. That is also how the sages described the Messianic Era, and the life to come. Hope springs eternal.

❖ Notes

CPSIA information can be obtained
at www.ICGtesting.com
Printed in the USA
LVHW091832250319
611761LV00003B/404/P

9 780827 614604